Praise for
Gently Falls Her Rain Of Light

"Lawrence Edwards has a unique and love drenched connection to the divine Mother as Kali. From this connection has flowed a stream of living holy water. A long unfurling tender revelation in poems of profound devotion and awe. His new book, while absolutely aware of Kali's savagery, celebrates the mystery behind that savagery. A mystery of burning tender transfiguring love. What deeper inspiration could we ask for in a time so threatened by nihilism and despair."
—**Andrew Harvey**, author of *The Return of the Mother; The Hope;* and *Radical Regeneration* with Carolyn Baker. www.andrewharvey.com

"This powerful collection of poems invites us to risk leaping off the edge of rational, binary knowing into the sacred Unknowing that lies around and within us. Turning from poem to poem becomes a dance conducted by the Lord and Mistress of eternal Love. *Gently Falls Her Rain of Light* resonates with the wisdom found in such mystics of East and West as Jesus, Buddha, Marguerite Porete, Julian of Norwich, Meister Eckhart, Thomas Merton, Ibn ʿArabī, Paramahamsa Yogananda, and Ramakrishna."
—**Dr. Robert A. Jonas**, Founder & Director of The Empty Bell, retreat leader, musician, environmental activist, and author: *My Dear Far-Nearness: The Holy Trinity as Spiritual Practice* and *The Essential Henri Nouwen* (editor). www.emptybell.org

Back in the 1970s the spiritual teacher known as Ram Das summed up the teachings on how to achieve enlightenment with the words "Be here now." The idea being that if you could, even for one instant, be absolutely, unconditionally in the present moment—in the

NOW—you would dissolve into the luminescent light of pure consciousness. Lawrence Edwards' beautiful and moving poetry in *Gently Falls Her Rain of Light* takes you into that moment and guides you on the journey to finding yourself—finding your true Self—in the radiant light and Oneness of All.

Each and every poem is an invitation from the Divine Feminine—pouring into and out of Lawrence—to enter into Union, into Wholeness, into the Oneness and radiance of the All. These poems contain so many moving images, so many deeply relevant insights, so many Truths, that it is almost impossible to pick out the most meaningful among them. And yet here are a few lines that, in their exquisite and utter simplicity, summed up for me the ineffable peace that can be found when one loses oneself in the lustrous light of the Beloved:

> *Take refuge in*
> *My loving embrace*
> *Rest in Beauty*
> *Rest in Grace.*

—**Teri Degler**, workshop leader and author of *The Divine Feminine Fire: Creativity And Your Yearning To Express Your Self* and *Gopi Krishna—A Biography: Kundalini, Consciousness, and Our Evolution to Enlightenment*. www.teridegler.com

Poetry often conveys truth better than any other form. In this book you will encounter beautiful words that shine with truth. The truth of love, the truth of surrender, and the truth of unity. Reading these poems with an open heart and mind you find yourself invited into an inner revolution that leads back to your original home. I would encourage anyone to savor these profound expressions of truth.

—**Jeff Carreira**, meditation and spirituality teacher, and author of *Transdimensional Spirituality*. www.jeffcarreira.com

Kalidas (Lawrence Edwards) guides the reader beyond tendencies to dwell in memory, confusion, and reactivity into the light of Divine Presence. This collection of treasures is filled with gems of insight, gold of wisdom, and beauty that reflects the faces of the Divine. Each poem is an invitation to embrace and dance with the Sacred.
—**Martin Lowenthal, PhD**, author of *Avatars of Wisdom, Love and Service* and *To Bless In Challenging Times: A Season Of Blessings.* https://dli.org/books

Lawrence Edwards continues to inspire. His poems are a secret window on the private moments of the meditating soul in communion with the Eternal in an ongoing dialog. Mother and child, lover and Beloved, self and the Self of selves. Throughout, the divine touch keeps returning to us as droplets trailing down windowpanes, the rain cascading down in torrents, manifesting for us the heavenly presence eternally circulating. Read these poems with openness and stillness. They awaken blissful moments.
—**Ivan Granger**, author of *The Longing In Between: Sacred Poetry From Around The World* and creator of the online sacred poetry site, Poetry Chaikhana—www.poetry-chaikhana.com.

These poems are pure gold! Nothing more need be said.
—**Lee Lyon**, author of *The 112 Meditations from the Book of Divine Wisdom: the meditations from the Vijnana Bhairava Tantra with commentary and guided practice,* Founder and Director of the Institute for Integrative Meditation. www.integrativemeditation.com

Gently Falls Her Rain Of Light

Collected by Kalidas

Offered by Lawrence Edwards, PhD

Published by TSJ Publications

ISBN paperback: 979-8-9874949-1-2
ISBN ebook: 979-8-9874949-2-9
Library of Congress Control Number: 2024905068

Om Namah Ganga Maa!
Cover Photo Credit: Steve Jurvetson
https://commons.wikimedia.org/wiki/File:Milky_Way_Night_
Sky_Black_Rock_Desert_Nevada.jpg
https://creativecommons.org/licenses/by/2.0/
Illustration: Rose Bindu by Molly Edwards
Photo: Rose & Frog, ©2022 Lawrence Edwards;
Maha Kali Yantra ©2005 Lawrence Edwards

Additional works by Lawrence Edwards:
The Soul's Journey: Guidance from the Divine Within
Awakening Kundalini: The Path To Radical Freedom
Kali's Bazaar penned by Kalidas
O My Beloved: Whisperings From The Divine Heard By Kalidas

For more information visit: www.thesoulsjourney.com

Dedication

To the Divine
In all Her forms!

Om Kali Ma!

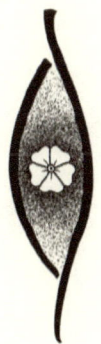

Contents

Preface

My dear reader,

This collection, *Gently Falls Her Rain Of Light*, was gathered by this leaky old vessel serving as best it can! Please forgive me, so much spillage! But, by Her grace, these gifts can be offered. Who is She? Ahhhhh, She is our Beloved, the Divine, who wears countless forms. She sprinkled them in my lap, usually during morning meditation, between the autumn of 2021 and the end of summer 2023. What She gives is so far beyond what words can convey, yet She lovingly demands the effort be made, the scribe must write, finding consolation in Her love for his failings to transmit what only Her Love, Her Grace, can impart.

The two previous collections of Her gifts, *Kali's Bazaar* and *O My Beloved,* originated in a similar way and serve to help people find the same source, the same wisdom and inspiration within themselves. It's been deeply moving for me to share Her gifts in a series of gatherings titled "Listening To The Divine Within." Participants discover their own insights and revelations invoked by the poetry, as Her gifts take everyone more deeply into their own divine nature and the grace unfolding in their lives. She wants us to know Her living presence is always here, now, everywhere.

May you find your way beyond the words into the silence, into Her pure heart of Love, the heart of God, beating within you even now. There Her Rain Of Light never ceases.

May you hear
God whispering in your ear
"I love you, I am you"
"I love you, I am you"
"I love you, I am you,"
as all your suffering
slips away.

In love and service,
Kalidas
Lawrence Edwards

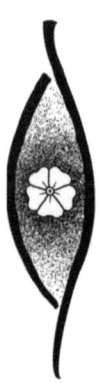

Gently falls Her rain of Light
The loving stream of Her voice
Warmly caressing the night,
O Sweet Voice of Darkness!
You alone fill my sight!

Morning Prayer

O my beloved
You awaken me to your living Presence
always here, now.
I feel your breath upon me,
I feel your breath within me,
You breathe me into existence.
You awaken me to your throbbing heart,
Love embracing all,
becoming all,
Love coursing through your body—all creation,
emanating from your loving heart,
all there is, is You.

Grant that I may remain awake
to Your living Presence
every moment throughout this day.

Grant that I may joyfully serve
and delight in all Your forms
that come to me today!

Grant that I may feel your breath
upon my neck, your arms embracing me,
our hearts pulsing as one.

Merge

In unwavering stillness,
Embraced by silence,
Sitting beside the
River's mouth
One hears
Ahhhhhhh . . .
As she merges
With the sea.

Here We Are

God is present
in every moment
in every heart.
O my Beloved,
here we are!
May I follow your
every step
in your wild
unfathomable
love dance!

The mind gnaws

The mind gnaws on the dry bones
of bygone experiences,
collects strings of stone-cold diamonds
it desperately cherishes,
running over and over them,
a mala of past consolations.
Even the rarest gem
emanates no light
in a darkened room.
Clinging to the past
blinds you to the brilliant
Presence of the Effulgent One
here and now.
Always here and now!

O mind,
ruminating on the past,
no matter how glorious,
separates you
from the Radiant One
here and now.
Your longing,
your spiritual thirst,
will not be satisfied
by mere memories
of yesterday's visitations.
Can you prepare a meal from
glossy pictures of last season's
luscious fruits and vegetables?

Will a video of that dinner
with friends last fall
diminish your hunger for the
sustenance you need now?

Relinquish past and future!
The Faceless One
continuously reveals
Her many facets
here and now!
Feast, dance, merge
with the Beloved
here and now!

Another turn round your ballroom?

O my Beloved,
You illuminated
who I am
and
who I am not.
Free from delusion
the truth of All
is clearly visible!
How can we ever
know another
when we don't know
our Self?
When we don't know
You!

Now you stand naked
everywhere I turn!
Matter, O Mater,
You!
You!
Only You!
Shakti, my Beloved,
pure energy
pure You
dancing everywhere!

Mind throbbing,
neurons pulsing,
brainwaves singing,
Consciousness humming—

All Shakti!
All You!
All wonder!
All delight!

O my Beloved dance partner,
You unfold
the eternity of time,
the infinitude of space,
Shall we take another turn
round Your ballroom?

Is

Is
Should be
Is
Should be
Is
Should be
Is
Should be
Is
Should be
Is
Should be
Is
Should be
Is

O mind,
Abandon this swing!
Sit on the throne
Of equanimity.
Your true home
Is the Palace of Peace.

Singing from the heart

Mind, coming to rest
in the vast stillness
born from the cessation
of all wants and needs,
hears the voice of the Divine
singing from the heart
of every being, so sublime,
humming in everything
living and non-living,
Ahhhhhhh
    Hummmm*
Ahhhhhhh
    Hummmm
Ahhhhhhh
    Hummmm
I AM
I AM
I AM

*AHAM is the ancient Sanskrit mantra, the sound form of the Divine that means "I AM," silently repeating itself day and night, Ahhhhhh as the breath comes in, Hummmm as the breath goes out.

Shiva

Wildly dancing,
Swirling faster
Faster! faster!
Shakti flying off
Like sparks in a gale
Roaring through
A blazing forest,
Swirling and twirling
Tighter and faster
The still point
Beckoning ever more
Insistently,
Cries of ecstasy
Shatter time
Exploding space herself
All forms released
Cosmic Fusion!
Infinite Shakti!
All is One!
All is One!
Shivo'ham!
Shivo'ham!*

*Ancient Sanskrit mantra: "I am the auspicious One."

O Buddha!

O Buddha!
Yes, you!
Wake up!
Now!

Buddha—fully awake and aware,
awake to the nature of life,
emotions, death, joy, suffering, love and compassion.
Awake to our infinite, radically free nature.

Meditation is the path of wakefulness.
Only one who is awake can steer the mind/body vehicle
in the direction of boundless joy, compassion and love.

Those who are asleep—caught in anger,
fear, jealousy, and greed
are like unconscious drunks driving their cars full speed
into other unconscious drunks driving their cars
along the rutted roads of existence,
creating tremendous suffering along the way,
until they finally cease at death
only to begin again with rebirth.

Wake up!
Now!
End the cycle!

Walk with awareness, fully awake,
and your every step will be one of freedom and peace.

Breathe with awareness, fully awake,
and your every breath will lead to freedom.

Eat with awareness, fully awake,
and with every mouthful you will savor
your Buddha nature.

Drink with awareness, fully awake,
and with every sip you will taste the joy of true peace.

Move through the world with awareness, fully awake,
and you will bring the blessings of love and compassion to all you
encounter.

Only one who is awake is free to choose
the way of Love in every moment.

Hari Om!*

Hari Om!
Who is the seer?
Who is the seen?
Who is the dreamer?
Who is the dream?
Two dissolves
into one.
One dissolves
into none.
If you want your Infinitude,
If you want boundless love
rapture, freedom . . .
surrender now!
Give up all concepts!
Give up all images!
Give up all thinking!
Give up all doing!
What you seek
is beyond all known existence.
Sacrifice all.
You cease to exist.
Pure Consciousness alone remains.

*Ancient Vedic mantra invoking the One who removes all sorrow, all suffering.

I see you

I see you.
You are myself as seeker.
You are myself as wanderer.
You are myself as confused.
You are myself as lost.
You are myself as pain.
You are myself as grief.
You are myself as anger.
You are myself as anguish.
You are myself as fear.
You are myself as hunger.
You are myself as longing.
You are myself as soul.
You are myself as lover.
I see you, all of you.
I love you.
I am you.
I am your Self blissfully free!

Knowing and unknowing

Knowing and unknowing,
    both are in the body of God.

You can turn your back
    on Sophia*,
        go blind . . .

But you can never leave
    the body of the Infinite One!
        Tat Twam Asi!**

*Sophia is the Goddess of Wisdom
**Ancient Vedic mantra: "Thou Art That."

Seeing the mind

Seeing the mind
as it is
it is a prism.

Not seeing the mind
as it is
it is a prison.

A Visitation

A nor'easter rages outside
As I sit in my little temple,
Rain pounding the roof.
Great sheets of rain,
Gathered by the wind,
Hurled through the forest,
Cascades of autumn leaves
Join the Great Mother's wild dance!

She's made Herself known
To even the most pitifully
Disconnected ones,
Though they only view Her
Insistent presence as another
Annoyance.
So tragically wrapped up
In their self-imprisoned existence,
They miss Her beauty, grace
And power unfolding in
Every moment,
Every element.

She is the tiny raindrop,
Unassuming,
Slowly coursing down
The window pane,
Without a hint of the
Miraculous journey
She has been on for
Eons beyond imagining.

Billions and billions and billions
Of years ago she took birth
In a star,
A nuclear furnace
Of Maa's creativity,
Transmuting energy
Into matter.
Then, in a truly cosmic,
Explosive orgasm,
A supernova,
She birthed all the elements into
Her universe of form
And emptiness.

Billions and billions
Of years later
She was pulled into
Our solar system.

Billions of years later
She fell to earth
Giving life to countless
Forms depending on her.
Rising and falling,
O so silently,
She continues
Age after age.

She fell from the sky,
Continuing her life-giving rounds.
Now, quietly sliding down my window,
Making her way once again

To the ground of all being,
Nurturing all from
Her hidden depths.

Her Voice

Her voice emanating from the Void,
Where only Truth resides,
Sings all into existence!
Refine your awareness,
Hear Her throbbing Consciousness!
Listen!
Listen to the stream of
Her voice,
Carrier wave of
All joy,
All delight,
All Love,
All Light!

Answering your call

O my Beloved,
Answering your call
I vanished!
Now, who is the caller
And who is the called?

Infinite blue sky

Infinite blue sky—
    clouds drift through unbounded space
Sun illumines all.

Trails Of Droplets

She spoke from the Void,
Her words,
Invisible rays of Shakti,
Coursing through the mind,
Leaving trails of droplets,
Thoughts coalescing in their chamber,
Pointing
Always pointing
Back to their
Source.

(The image of the first time I saw a Wilson cloud chamber revealing hidden realities in a university physics course came to mind with this poem.)

Radiating from the Void

Radiating from the Void
Subtle blue light
Pierces the eternal night
Essence of Consciousness
Intensifying
All pervasive
All-becoming Light
All-embracing Love
Coalescing
Pulsing, throbbing,
Shimmering Being!
Shimmering Becoming!
Shimmering Existence!
Shimmering all there is!
All there is—
Shimmering Love!
Hari Om!

Dancing

Dancing through the sky—
    metallic red dragonfly
Lands! Tickles finger!

She winked!

I dreamt of Lord Vishnu
 Ocean of Consciousness
  Dreaming the Cosmos

Shree Padma, Para Shakti,
 Sat unmoving
  Creating all!

Revealing that,
 She looked at me
  And winked!

Who is the dreamer?
Who is the dream?

It's a dance!

It's a dance!
All of life!
Shiva Nataraj showing the way!
We so often feel compelled to say NO to things we've been bound to
in order to repossess our power to consciously and fully say YES!
Yes as an empowered choice,
not a conditioned pattern forcing itself on us.

Our life unfolds as the Divine within the Divine.
There's nowhere to go, nothing to escape,
Nothing to possess
that you don't already have in abundance beyond imagining!
In this love-play, love-dance, we call life,
we put on different robes,
which are energized and made radiant
by the heart of Love just beneath the robe!
The mind confuses itself with the robe,
the role, the character,
summoned in the moment to play its part,
but freedom comes from knowing
you are the actor, the dancer,
bringing love and attention to the part
you're given in your family, your community,
and your wonderful dharmic work.
Delight in the dance!
Know the bliss of Shivo'ham—I Am Shiva!
I Am The Auspicious One!
I am the Lord of the Dance!
Know the bliss of freedom!

Wake up to the nature of mind

Wake up to the nature of mind,
struggling against raging currents,
tumbled, tossed by turbulence,
its own creation,
flailing about vainly convincing itself
of its power and control,
it goes blind
to the hall of mirrors it scurries about in,
fleeing fires of fear,
anger, and hunger.
Where is its escape?
Where is the fire exit?

My dear one,
drop it!
Drop it all!
The only reality it has
is the reality you give it.
Surrender!
Fall!
Fall into stillness.
Surrender to your Divine Source!
Fall into the luscious silence
    of the Divine embrace.
All the mind's projected tortures evaporate.
Only the Infinite, beyond words remains.

Deep Longing—The Mystics' Way

We too often live
in a state of deprivation,
deep longing buried
beneath layers of resignation
and inadequate accommodations
that can't dispel our soul's anguish.

Softening the inner fortress we've built
to shield us from the profound pain
we've been told we must endure,
told we deserve,
told there's no escape from,
told to sacrifice our sacred gifts,
even our lives to,
to the vision of the ruling powers
who built the cross on which we
hang in agony . . .
softening, we search.

We turn to religion
and we're treated as
unruly, undisciplined
knaves needing to be
forcibly trained out
of our state of toxic ignorance.
Desperate for relief,
we fall to our knees
in obedience to spiritual tyrants
the same way fear-driven citizens,
hoping for relief,

give in to political despots and oligarchs.
When the predators in power
control myths and religions,
the people accepting those delusions
willingly obey their
treacherous self-serving leaders.

Even the grace-filled gifts
of enlightened ones,
avatars, sages and saints,
Christ, Buddha, Mohammed . . .
in the hands of predators
become weapons, prisons,
and brutal barriers of exclusion.

Is not our state of anguish,
our oft denied state of desperation,
a natural response to
our deprivation?
To our soul deadening,
relentlessly exploiting,
materialist society?
How we've been enculturated
to seek relief through
consumption and competition
serves those in power,
but our hearts and souls
are tortured and starved.
Don't blame yourself
for not being nourished by
the toxic gruel that is offered.
Those blinded by power
always blame their victims.

The pain and anguish can
point to what we really need.

*First, step away from the
conditioned mind.*

Patiently, listen deeply to your heart.

The grace-filled missives
from the holy mystics
who have gone beyond
all dogmas and religions
hint at how to look within
for genuine answers,
for ineffable Truths,
for the direct knowing
that has always threatened
religious and secular authorities.

Mystics are revolutionaries.
You are a mystic.
Throw off the bonds
of convention,
of collective delusion!

Dare to ask yourself
How fully, completely
Loved do I feel every day?
O you dear sweet soul,
you deserve that every moment
of every day!
The Divine within you is radiating
that love right here, right now, always!

Turn to the Source
for what you need.

Ask yourself, how have my heart and soul
been loved and nurtured,
and had their inherent worth
reflected back to them from the time
I was conceived?
What did I learn
about lovingly nourishing myself
and others every day?
Has my mind been loved
and cared for in ways
that nourish it
and strengthen it
to lovingly know and to selflessly serve?
Has my body been lovingly
touched, appreciated, respected,
and cared for
as often as it genuinely needs?

What we give loving attention to
flourishes, all else withers.

Watch where your attention goes.
Exercise your power to step out of rote
patterns of giving attention and love
in ways that don't serve the truth
of who you are
and who others are
as emanations of the Divine.

As a mystic you reclaim the vision
of the Divine unfolding as all creation,
including and embracing you and your life.
You are empowered to
act in accord with that deep truth.
This is how mystics come to be
viewed as revolutionaries.
Material ambitions and success
never meet the anguished cries
of our souls in need of the
Divine's embrace.

The graceful hints
and practices passed on
by mystics for thousands of years
serve as starting points,
not endpoints.

Direct knowing unfolds
in the sacred vessel
of your heart,
the true holy grail,
the temple wherein the
Divine has always dwelt.

Lovingly engage in practices,
meditation, contemplation, seva—
Always lovingly!
Meditation is the state of
pure all-embracing love,
unity beyond any concept of unity.

Don't bring a stick to your practice.

Wrap yourself in a soft shawl
to remind yourself you are
enveloped in Love.
Wrap the mind in a shawl of
wonder, gratitude, love and awe,
as you sit in the Divine Presence.
Here, you are lovingly invited
to let go and let go,
let go and let go
into that Love.

Choose love moment by moment.
Choose love and you've chosen God.

That's what it means to put God
above all else.
Put Love above all!
The mind will eventually discover
what all mystics discover,
the inexhaustible wellspring of Love,
already within you,
will fill you forever.

What's tucked inside the night

What's tucked inside the night
  Can never be found by day.
What's hidden in plain sight
  Will never lead you astray.

Not even emptiness

Shed all your clothes, my friend
All cloaks you've adorned yourself with
must go.
You've been called
by no one.
No one alone
can answer.
Not this, not that,
All this, all that,
Swaha!
Not even emptiness
remains.
You won't find
what you seek
in scriptures,
nor in churches, temples,
or mosques.
Not gazing at the heavens,
the ocean, or sublime forms.
Certainly not behind your eyelids, nor
on the floor in front of you!
Give up, give it all up!
Every effort betrays
your ignorance.
You cling to separation
while crying for union.
Give up, give it all up,
two
one
none
gone

O *The Sweet Voice*

May you enter the stillness
The silence
The Divine Presence.

O the sweet voice
of Darkness
whispering,
even now whispering . . .

May you hear,
hear God,
so close, so intimately near,
now whispering
whispering in your ear,
"I love you, I am you."
"I love you, I am you."
"I love you, I am you,"
as all your suffering
slips away.

Walk

Walk the indescribable love-road
Through the ineffable field
Of Self-luminous Awareness
Where traveler, traveling and destination merge
In the Heart of the One!

Gazing At The Eternal

The ephemeral gazes
At the Eternal
Awash with wonder,
Awe and longing.

Go!
Go more and more deeply
Into the ocean of revelation!
Awe!
Wonder!
Longing!
O the lifetimes of longing . . .

These are Her invitations!
Go!
Go deeply, fully . . .
Dissolve the ephemeral
In the eternal!

I and Thou
Merging beyond all!
Rapture beyond rapture!
Nothing remains.
Swaha!

Thich Nhat Hanh

O Beloved Thay,
Though you've never left
Please return quickly!

Mother Earth misses
The soft touch
Of your peaceful
Steps.

The wind misses
Caressing your radiant
Loving face.

The Darkness
Cries out in agony
For the living flame
Of your luminous
Compassion.

May our hearts
Our bodies
Our minds
Carry your living presence
Of boundless loving kindness
To all beings.

May we breathe in
Discord, as you have,
And breathe out
Only peace.

O Beloved Thay,
Though you've never left
Please return quickly!

Lovely little snowflake

Ahhhh . . . lovely little snowflake
gracefully falling,
the world hushed
by your beauty,
sky-dancer delivering
your crystal radiance
to the earth.
In you, dear snowflake,
we see the ocean
from which you arose,
the moon, tides and currents,
we see the clouds
you became, urged by the luminous one
to fly across earth and sea,
your path has taken you
into the ground, then
carried you aloft in a tree,
only to descend to ground
once again as an
autumn leaf!
Mother earth carries you
to a stream, a river,
finally, back into the sea.

O beloved snowflake,
you reveal all creation
in your humble presence,
and the love and delight
of the Creator, too!
You lie on the earth

outside my window,
hinting at stars long gone,
sparkling now in the sun,
urged by its warmth
to dissolve your sacred geometry,
sinking into Mother earth
you help her nurture
all the life she carries.

When the Infinite

When the Infinite
and the finite
meet,
When the One
and the many
merge,
Love is truly
known.

Spring!

Light and life growing,
    warm rain gets peepers peeping!
Bullfrogs croak bass notes!

River of grace

River of grace
My Beloved's face
Let go, let go
Rest in Her flow
Let go, let go
Rest in Her flow
Let go, let go
Rest in Her flow . . .

This Beggar

O my Beloved,
I hear your voice
calling me from beyond
the beyond,
beyond all . . .
your voice—
currents of silent
sound
rays of radiant
darkness
bridge into your Being,
    the unfathomable enormity
        of you holding the universe
            like a lustrous pearl.
You—beauty beyond beauty,
Truth beyond truth,
Wisdom beyond wisdom,
Mystery beyond mysteries—
You send me away babbling!
Who will believe the gifts you offer
    when this beggar returns
empty-handed?
What is there to grasp?
What can hold your
    Luminous Presence!
        Your inexhaustible Grace!
        Your boundless Love!

Listen my friend,
Give up!
Surrender now!
Dissolve back into Her,
Source of all!

.

You were propelled

O Mind,
You were propelled
    into existence,
Born from Mother's
    womb.
You fought to own
    your independence.
The self-born separation
    has left you longing,
searching
    for the boundless ocean
        of Love you remember
            swimming in.

That blissful ocean buoys
    your every thought
        your every breath
            your every heartbeat.
Now, in profound stillness
    you sense the Ocean of Love
        in which you have unknowingly
            swum for eons.

Ancient threads of fear
    bind you, O mind.
Your hard-won individuality,
    so easily threatened,
        ensnares you,

Pulling against the irresistible urge
    to dissolve back into
        Mother's embrace,

Not knowing that it has been
    Her will, Her grace,
        that has created the
Entire field
    in which you play!

Struggle, succeed, fail,
    live and die,
All Her
All Her
All Her
Your entire existence
All Her!

To all the Beloved said

To all the Beloved said,
"Take refuge in
My loving embrace
rest in beauty
rest in grace."

A sweet little being
hearing Her gentle voice
found comfort and rest
at long last.

Photo credit: ©2022 Lawrence Edwards

The dawning of radiant mind

The dawning of radiant mind
The blossoming of love sublime
Luminous effulgence all-pervading
Not one, not two, all-erasing!

Quick my Love

Quick my Love,
your quiver is full!
Shoot!
Shoot now!
My heart aches!
Shoot your love-arrows now
for this beggar's sake!
Pierce my heart,
spill this Love,
my heart's life-blood
at your feet!

Pierce my heart
again and again!
Your ecstatic love-arrows
are all I need!
Let my heart gush love
'til all is gone
offered at your feet.

The sun that never sets

The sun that never sets
has dispelled all
clouds of ignorance.
Illuminating the
four states
with blissful wisdom,
Love envelopes all.
All am I.

Poor impoverished mind

Poor impoverished mind,
you suffer and complain
you chase one mirage
after another
seeking fulfillment
in emptiness.
You are a fish in the ocean
complaining of thirst!
You are made of the same
infinite energy that dances
in countless forms within
and without!
How can you lack energy
for becoming free?
How can you whine about
not having power?
At root you are the unimpeded power
of freedom—Swatantrya Shakti!
Wake up from this delusion!
Realize your effortless natural state
of boundless Consciousness
radiant with infinite love, wisdom,
stillness and ecstasy!
Know this and you will tirelessly
endeavor to set all beings
free from suffering!

Emaho!*

*Tibetan Buddhist saying: "so may it be!"

O little bubble

O little bubble
You are always in the
    Ocean of Her
Boundless Being,
Boundless Knowing,
Boundless Love.
Invited now to
Dissolve and remember,
Dissolve and re-emerge
Awake!
Awake to Her Play!
Awake to being Her playmate!
Her Beloved!
Her Spouse!
Awake!
Awake Now!
Beyond two!
Beyond one!
Beyond beyond!

I met a teacher

I met a teacher
on the road today.
I was walking by the lake
and an earthworm
was making her way
across the pavement.
We hung out together
for a while.
It had rained,
she was above ground
waiting for her home
to dry out enough
to return.
I have had floods
in my home,
so we commiserated!
She told me her
family was from Europe.
Mine, too, I said!

So we're both invaders, she said.
Someone told
us that long ago.
What's an invader, anyway?
Sometimes the guilt
is so painful.
How far back
does one have to go
to find non-invaders?

I don't know
I tell her.
I suppose,
as Einstein said,
it's all relative.

Is Einstein a relative
of yours? she asked.

Well, some things are
lost on worms.
Invaders are unwelcome
dominating interlopers
who take
what belongs to
those who are
already there.
You're such a humble
creature, how did
you conquer
a continent?

I have no idea,
don't know what
a continent is,
don't know what
a Europe is!
she said.
We just eat all we can
and have as many kids
as possible.

Everything else
just happens.
Do you think there's a larger plan
that we don't control?

Dear earthworm,
you are more
intuitive than you
are given credit for!
My earthy friend,
did you know
people have gotten
doctoral degrees
studying your family?

What's a degree?

Let's not get into
that can of . . .
well, let's not get into
that, now!
It's supposed to
indicate a level
of mastery.

Mastery of us?
she asked.

No, just information
about you.

Oh.

I think you
deserve an honorary
doctoral degree
in humility, I said.

I need to go back
underground
before I'm eaten!

Well said my
humble friend!
Thank you for your
grounded wisdom!

Why do you wander the world

My dear friend,
why do you wander the world
empty, begging bowl in hand,
knocking on doors
of bankrupt fools?
What do you expect they will have?
They've given you pity and scorn,
crumbs of praise
for piety you don't own.
Your sincere deluded efforts
carry the fragrance
of true love and longing.
Turn,
Turn within,
Discover where true love
and deep longing arise.
There, set down your bowl.
The One has been waiting
to fill it to overflowing,
spilling out pure Love
through all the sense portals,
flooding the world!
O beggar friend,
you are on the brink,
let go
let go into the emptiness
that is the fullness
of the One alone!

The One

The One
wishing to know
two, three, four . . .
created mind
like a prism.
Unity Consciousness
passing through
the differentiating mind
appears as countless forms
including the form
of individuality
of self . . .

Yet the One remains
unbroken
undifferentiated
in the midst
of differences
It sees only One
only Self.

It is the One
illuminating itself
as multiplicity.
Without Its radiance
even the sun
would disappear
in darkness.
Consciousness is
the substratum
of all existence.

As the One
we behold all
as our Beloved Self.

As mind
we behold
otherness
everywhere.

Mystics
returning to Source
passing upstream
through the mind
return to Unity Consciousness
eternally present—
Source and substance
of all appearances.

Beholding Self
everywhere
everything
every being
all Self,
we dissolve
in love drenched
ecstasy!

Jai Maa!*

*Hail or Victory to the Great Mother!

Life is the unfolding of the Divine

Life is the unfolding of the Divine,
the Infinite,
in Its field of time and space.

All forms are the unfolding of the Divine,
the Infinite,
in Its field of time and space.

We are the unfolding of the Divine,
the Infinite,
in Its field of time and space!

Grace, Its power of revelation,
illumines all
moment by moment
to one free of self.
Take refuge in Grace
and know
Infinite
Joy!

Mind, be prepared

Coursing through deep prajnaparamita* . . .
Mind, be prepared.
All coming
All going
Cease.
Not one
Not two.
No inside
No outside.
No emergence
No dissolution.
No going
No gone
No savritti
No nivritti.
All as all.
All forms
No forms
All as all.
Consciousness and
Ecstasy gone.
Beloveds
Gone.
All as all
All beyond all.
Beyond beyond
No beyond.
No time
No space
No past

No present
No future.

All time
All space
All universes
A dimensionless

•

Gone.
Swaha!

*perfect transcendental wisdom beyond the mind

Sweet Voice Of Darkness

In the depths of night
An open window
Allowed the sweet voice
Of Darkness
To pour over the sill
Onto the floor
Gradually flooding the room
With Her presence.
Floating me off my bed,
The warm waves of Her
Singing, carrying me
Through Her portal
Beyond . . .
Indescribably beyond . . .
Her song of love
Birthing universes
Birthing you
A song within Her song.

Death

It is one of the most challenging
situations we face in life,
the slow
torturous
process
of a loved one dying,
my beloved sister dying,
the ravages of cancer unstoppable.

To be fully present
is to be in a cloud of grace,
a soft luminous light of Love . . .
holding and being held . . .
nothing left out,
One in Love.

Her body surrendered
To the relief Lord Yama offered.
Her Light and Love
Continue unbounded.

Coursing through deep prajnaparamita

Coursing through deep prajnaparamita
The clear, self-luminous expanse
    Of boundless Awareness . . .

Ahhhh . . . the play of forms
    arising and subsiding . . .

Emptiness within emptiness
    Nothing
    blissfully appearing
    as everything . . .

Aham
    Ahhhhhh . . .

(Om in Sanskrit ॐ has the crescent moon shape above which is the dot, the bindu. Together they symbolize going beyond name and form, dissolving into the bindu, womb and tomb of all creation, the portal beyond all names, all forms. Om emerges from the bindu and dissolves back into it, as does all creation—including you.)

Who Can Say What I'm Not

Chant

Om Taré Tuttaré Turé Soha (3X)
AHAM!
I AM!
I am Tara!
I am Kwan Yin!
I am Mother Mary!
I am Inanna!
I am Shekinah!
AHAM!
I AM!

I am Kali!
I am Shakti!
I am Saraswati!
I am Parvati!
I am Sundari!
AHAM!
I AM!

Who can say
What I'm not!
Neti neti
Iti Iti
Shivo'ham
HAMSA!

I AM!
AHAM!
I AM!
AHAM!
I AM!
AHAM!

(To hear Lawrence chanting this visit:
https://youtu.be/H_4EQztqmV4.)

Radiant Silence

She shed all cloaks,
every thread of attachment,
every thought of self,
dissolving into the velvet blackness
beyond being
and non-being.
Shimmering silence . . .
Radiant silence . . .
Boundless ocean of silence . . .
Embracing her,
erasing all separation.
Only the Infinite expanse
of Love,
Eternal Presence . . .
Radiant Stillness . . .
Is all,
All
that truly exists.

O Great Mother

O Great Mother,
You alone
are the seeker
and the sought,
the teacher
and the taught.
Playing at two
but always You.

Come

Come my dear,
Come to rest
In the Divine embrace,
Here at last
All fears
All pain
Are fully erased.

Encountering The Infinite

Encountering the Infinite,
the Dark One,
The mind falls into silence
Like no silence it has ever known.

Not the silence of sleep,
Nor unconsciousness,
Not the foggy quiet of self-absorption,
But absolute silence—
Magnificent,
Terrible,
Overwhelming—
The silence of pure awe,
of self-erasing rapture.

Enter the presence of the One
and feel the mind
extinguished,
blissfully annihilated,
replaced
by infinite
All-embracing Love.

Full Moon

The recent full moon poured her light into my bedroom window the other night. Perhaps you, too, received some of her wondrous gifts!

I remember as a small child the delight of discovering the moon followed me wherever I went. I would watch it racing behind trees to keep up with our car as my father drove us home at night. When we came to a wide-open field or expanse of sky, dear moon would slow to a stately pace more befitting such a grand presence!

When we arrived home, it didn't matter if I turned my back on the moon and ran ahead, suddenly jumping and turning around—there she was, right behind me. As I ran into the house and dashed from window to window, there she was—even if I ran upstairs, I'd find her peeking in the window!

Many years later, my path took me into the uncharted wilderness of a liminal world. I came upon a clearing in the high mountain forests where a marvelous spring welled up from far beneath the mountain, creating a clear, deep, pool of water nourishing life all around it.

Feeling extremely thirsty, I plunged my face into the water, drinking it in. The water was more than mere water! It quenched more than one's thirst. It brought a stillness to the very source of thirst, of want, of need, of any kind of restlessness. In that sublime stillness my awareness rested, whole and complete in every way—effortless, living, breathing meditation.

Regardless of whether my eyes were open or closed, there was boundless stillness, boundless spaciousness, boundless Light of awareness illuminating all.

The pool's surface was like glass. Now and again a bird or deer would come and drink the same waters. At the far end of the pool was a waterfall where the spring water flowed over rocks before disappearing underground, becoming the hidden source of countless streams and rivers below.

Like ripples on a pond, the thought moved through my mind that I would have to leave this place. I took another draught of the living water and its purity stilled my mind once again. It was clear that the dharma of those who found their way to one of these divine wellsprings was to invite everyone to drink as well. Gazing at the still surface of the pool, it became a disc of Light—cool, shimmering, radiant light.

Back in this world I discovered this Light is always present, whether I've turned my attention towards it or away, there it is illuminating all. It doesn't matter if we think we've turned our back on it and lost it forever; simply turning one's attention back to its source reveals the Light to always be there for you, in you, as you, and more.

You can play hide-and-seek with it, like a child playing with the moon.

And you can plunge into the liquid embrace of the Light, feel the stillness, the tranquility, and the expansive presence of simply Being.

Being fully you.

Being unbounded, spacious, all-embracing, free.

Emaho!

Mind, you're choking

Mind,
you're choking on sand
dying of thirst
lost in an oasis mirage
in a desert of thoughts
longing
longing for the waters
of love and wisdom,
deluded by philosophies
and religion
you've become as brittle
as last autumn's leaves.
Even your contracted state
of hunger and thirst
is part of the bound mind's fate!

Sip the nectar of
Shivo'ham! Shivo'ham!
I am Infinite!
I am One!

Wake up to Reality!
You exist only in the ocean of
Saraswati's* graceful body!

Boundless love, wisdom, and rapture
are Her very nature!
Your very nature!

Expand once again!
Your tender juicy heart
embraces all!

Love dissolves
all that seemed so disparate,
so discordant
so other
in the unshakable peace of
One.

*Saraswati—"She who flows"—one of the most ancient names for
the Great Goddess, Mother of All.

You dear, dear soul

You dear, dear soul,
let go of all this efforting,
let go of all this collecting,
let go of all this grasping,
slip into the warm pool
of all-embracing Love
forever within you.
The inexhaustible wellspring
of the Divine fills your heart.
Pull aside the veil,
slide in!
Its peaceful waters invite you
to float in God's embrace.

Luminous Stillness

O my Beloved
the pervasiveness of suffering,
so hard for awakening souls to bear,
what are they to do?

My dear one,
pain is an exacting teacher.
For the ignorant
asleep to Reality
avoidance of pain
born of primal ignorance
drives their lives
from birth
to death
birth to death . . .

For those who remain still,
awake to the nature of pain,
Awareness illumines
the limits of pain

illumines the infinitude
within which the transient
experience of pain
arises and subsides

illumines the conditions
which give rise to pain

illumines the one identified
with the experience of pain

illumines the boundlessness
of radiant Awareness
suffused with rapturous Love
that encompasses it all.

Those who are waking
to Reality
need to take refuge in stillness,
abide in unshakeable peace,
repeatedly dissolve in the eternal
until they know the ineffable
Reality
beyond pleasure and pain
freedom and bondage
duality and non-duality
where only
luminous Love exists—
there is no other.

There is no freedom
from suffering
without abiding
in this state
of Being.

Until then
pain and those
who have traversed the way
beyond the way

teach you
to persevere,
diving ever deeper
into the luminous stillness of
effulgent infinite Awareness.

Let your mind rest in God

Let your mind rest in God
like your weary head surrendering
to the cool soft comfort of your
pillow at day's end.

Let your body rest in God
like an exhausted lover
surrendering to sleep
in the arms of her beloved.

Let your feet rest in God
like standing barefoot on a carpet of moss
in a lush forest
feeling the support of the earth
alive with the roots of countless trees drawing
vitality from the depths
while projecting heartwood and branches skyward
brushing the Infinite spaciousness of creation.

Mind and body at rest in the One,
Awareness—boundless, spacious, free
You
You are all this,
Rest,
Simply Be.

No matter

No matter how dazzling
the sun's reflection
in a humble mirror
or in polished gold
it's still just a reflection.

Student
seek the source
of the teacher's
illumination
not mere reflections.

Hidden

O my Beloved
How could I be
so dense and beguiled,
lifetimes of chasing after
one desire or another
not knowing
You've hidden yourself
in all desires!

It took eons
to fully understand
that no matter what desire
I filled
empty I remained.
Your trick is creating the illusion
that satisfying the want
would fill the cup of the soul.

You endowed the soul
with the wisdom to know
its deep thirst will never be
quenched by even the most
extraordinary possessions.
My soul's profound longing
turned out to be You
leading me across eons of time
before I could even discern
in the anguished depths
of emptiness
that it is You,

You are all I need
You are all I want
You are that burning ache
driving me through
countless births
countless worlds
to discover
there's nowhere to go
nothing to achieve
no one to become.

No
You demand the impossible.
Impossible applies only
to mind and body!
You require You alone
to release me
from the bondage
You created
delivering me into
Your loving embrace.
O my Beloved
bestower of grace,
You are one tricky Lady!

O Tarama

O Tarama, Divine Mother,
The world is ablaze with peoples'
fiery projections,
misery and suffering inflame
everyone's afflictions,
seeing otherness and
casting blame
the mind descends,
anger and hate set it aflame.

Taking responsibility for
their own state
the wise dispel
anger and hate
having seen them
arising from within
born of ignorance and delusion,
blaming others
only prolongs confusion.

Seeing the true cause of suffering
afflicting the mind
they free themselves
for the benefit all beings, every kind.

O my beloved candle

O my beloved candle,
your sweet warm glow
transforms the darkest night.
You never care how deep
the darkness is,
how dense the shadows,
you happily illuminate all
with your living flame,
quietly teaching any
who become still enough
to rest in your company,
their gaze absorbing
your radiant gifts.

Portals

O my Beloved
You are the portal
You are the infinite
You are the finite
You are beyond
both and neither.

As portal
You appear as a
gateway between
the ephemeral
and the eternal.
Where will your lovers,
seeking to dissolve
in You alone,
longing for You alone,
find Your portal?

My dear one,
reducing all desires
to one
frees the mind
from distractions.
This is
one-pointed mind.
This reveals
every moment
is a portal.
Now
Is the first
portal entered.

One-pointed mind
abiding solely
in the present
graced by Me
passes into
the four gated city

drawing nearer
to My portal
opening to
its source.

Having left
all doing behind,
abiding ever more deeply
in stillness,
in grace,
becoming more subtle
than empty space

pervading atoms
molecules, galaxies . . .
consciousness freed
from form
glides through
clouds of energy
active, leaden
and quiet,
becoming nothing,
ineffable stillness
pervades.

Only grace
can reveal
the final dissolution
passing through
the sacred portal
bindu
Me
revealing the
no-thingness
of no mind
beyond all words
of any kind,
Love beyond love
Rapture beyond telling.
Your Beloved's embrace
always awaits!

served. View the original on most of the videos on https://www.you tube.com/@AnamCaraMeditation and www.thesoulsjourney.com. A yantra is a visual form of the Divine, a portal to the Infinite. This yantra appeared as pure light to Lawrence in meditation, a gift of Ma Kali. She told him to paint it, though he had never painted before, and also told him the meaning of the various elements of the yantra. The four gated city is made up of the 2 lines forming the box around the flaming lotus. The two lines symbolize the past and future which must be left behind. To even enter the sacred precinct of Kali one must be fully present now. Each element of the yantra has symbolic meaning pointed to in this poem. The flaming petals are the clouds of energy which must be crossed to reach the essence of the three gunas, the three qualities represented by the 3 circular lines, which are then transcended. Enter the black void and confront the five concentric downward pointing triangles, symbols of the Great Goddess, where deeper mysteries are encountered. The bindu, the central black dot, is the most sacred portal of all, at the very heart of Maha Kali's yantra. Entering that, you and all creation cease to exist.

Dearest seeker

Dearest seeker,
My beloved Self,
The flame of Love
Illumines the cave
Of your heart.
Don't let it
Gutter out unseen
At your death.
Offer your life
To the living flame
  of Love
Offer every morsel you eat
To the living flame
  of Love
Offer every breath
To the living flame
  of Love
Offer every thought
To the living flame
  of Love
Offer all that you see
Hear, taste, touch
to the living flame
  of Love!
AAAAAAEEEEEEEEEEEE!

This is why you took birth!
You are the wick!
You are the flame!
You are the offering

Alight in the Name!
You are the blazing fire
    of Love
The effulgent Presence
    of the One!
Set the world ablaze
O living flame of Love!

Where are you looking?

Seeker,
Where are you looking?
Do you know where the
    Living Flame awaits you?
Don't be distracted by
    robes and hats!
Worship only the ONE!
The living Presence of
    the Divine
Blazes in your heart!
Take refuge there!
The Light and Love
    of God illumines
        all from within.

Look in the mirror

Look in the mirror
What do you see?
Aham Brahmasmi!*
Aham Brahmasmi!
The world is a mirror
What do you see?
Aham Brahmasmi!
Aham Brahmasmi!
Your heart is a mirror
What do you see?
Aham Brahmasmi!
Aham Brahmasmi!

*Ancient Vedic mantra—"I Am The Absolute."

Eclipse

Earth hides the full moon
    night's darkness gently deepens
Creatures find refuge.

Mahadevi

The throb of Her Presence
Her pulse of Love
Pervading every moment,
Pervading everybody,
    your body is Her body!
Pervading every life,
    your life is Her life!
All this—all Her!

This is what we long to know.
This is what we must know.

Stop fighting over crumbs
    the hungry mind, lost in ignorance,
        clings to.
The abundance of the Infinite One is
    always here, now!
Jai Maa!

Summoned

Silent night
Holy night
Moon so bright
Heart of Light

She's returned, but not as she was.

Some nights ago, in the darkest hours she felt it again, the urgent call summoning her to the forest edge. Leaving the warmth of her little cottage she ventured out, not knowing what was calling her or where it would take her. The full moon cast other-worldly shadows as she crossed the meadow to the wall of trees and underbrush.

"How will I know where to enter?" she thought, while skirting the dense forest. She kept telling herself to feel, to open deeply to simply feeling the summons, feel the opening, feel the presence she had felt in meditation. She felt she was getting closer, but was she? Then she felt the distinct pull to turn left into the woods. Right there was a barely visible opening, so small she had to enter on her knees.

In the thick forest the moonlight only faintly illumined her way. No human trails were here, just the narrow paths of wild things at home in the forest. Their calls and rustling surrounded her. Quieting her mind and body, she felt into the darkness of unknowing, unseeing, simply feeling the summons, letting it lead her blindly farther and farther into the thickening night woods, until she sensed a massive presence ahead of her.

The winding trails of the beasts led her to the base of an enormous mountain. Still the summons tugged at her heart, urging her on. Traversing the path along the base of the sheer wall of the mountain she could discern no entry. The moonlight was brighter here, but all she could follow was the feeling, the irresistible feeling of being drawn into the mountain itself. Cloaked in darkness, a huge, towering slab of the mountain that had fallen eons ago lay leaning against the mountain wall. A narrow opening between it and the mountain beckoned her. Leaving behind the moonlight, she entered and found the small hidden opening of a cave. The summons strengthened. Clearly she had to enter here.

The mouth of the cave was blacker than night. Bowing low to cross the threshold she continued; the cave narrowing even more as it descended. Before long she was on her hands and knees crawling through the blackness with only the powerful feeling of being summoned to guide and accompany her. Her knees began bleeding from crawling on the rock floor of the tunnel. The summons beckoned more strongly, empowering her to continue regardless of pain, hunger, or thirst.

After some hours, abruptly the tunnel ended. Another impenetrable wall of stone met her hands as they groped in the absolute darkness to feel a way forward. She felt no opening, nothing but some cracks in the stone wall and floor of the cave. There was a curious warmth down here. She sat in the utter darkness, facing the wall, feeling the warmth rising from the floor and radiating from the wall. There was no way forward. No going back. The call was stronger than ever.

She knew what she needed to do.

Nothing.

Absolutely nothing.

She had faced what seemed like insurmountable obstacles before in her life. Her master had taught her to enter the depths of stillness at these times and wait. So, she did. Her breath slowed and deepened. It became entrained to the deep throb emanating so very faintly from the heart of the mountain. There she sat. Empty of all thought, all imagining, all longing, all sense of self—she dissolved into the throbbing heart of the mountain.

What happened next can barely be spoken of, so sacred it is, so beyond language. Her body remained where it sat. The summons revealed the summoner, beyond words, beyond description, beyond time. It drew her into its infinitely loving embrace, revealing their eternal unity, their ecstasy, their beating heart of all creation, all existence, all life, all beings. The throb of the Infinite. That throb of Love is all there is. Its unfathomable delight in becoming all, becoming you, is beyond words.

None can say what became of her.

When

When the mind ceases
to indulge its fantasies
of who others are
it is ready to know
the Truth of who they are.

When the mind ceases
to indulge its fantasies
of who you are
it is ready to know
the Truth of who you are.

When the mind ceases
to indulge its fantasies
of who it is
it is ready to know
the Truth of what it is.

When the mind ceases
to indulge its fantasies
of who I AM
it is ready to know
the Truth of all that is.

Evil

Ignorance and fear
Spread by power-hungry ones
Make easy prey of those
Mired in struggles
Wrought by those insatiable exploiters.

Naïve seeker

The naïve seeker
Caught by hats and robes
Of convention
Adoring monuments
And temples
Of past revelations
Misses the master,
One who has become nothing
Looks like nothing,
Quietly walking through
The bazaar unnoticed.

Luscious and unblemished

Luscious and unblemished
The ripe fruit falls
Now all can enjoy!

The mind's delusions

The mind's delusions
Clouds forming and dissolving
I am this, I am that
Inner ghosts of past impacts
Like imprisoning craters,
I'm not this, I'm not that
Collective delusions, too
Religious, philosophical, economic, political
What won't the mind identify with
Creating illusory worlds
Which it will kill
To defend?
O pathetically bound mind
You truly are the source of suffering.
You are a king wearing the rags
Of a starving desperate thief.
Deluded by ignorance
You ravage the world.
Take refuge in the Love
Of your adoring Queen.
She has been seeking you
Across lifetimes!
Seeking to set you free!
Her throb of Love is resounding
Throughout the universe!
Broadcasting the truth of who you are!
Hear the call of Love!
Take refuge in that throb of Love.
It will cleanse you of all delusion.
Take refuge in the name of your Beloved

Om Kali Ma
Om Kali Ma
Om Kali Ma
Come home at last
To the truth of who you are.

Look Up!

No mud no lotus
No mud no lotus
No mud no lotus
Very nice!
Now, look up!
What illumines
mud and lotus?
No sun, no mud, no lotus.
The Self-luminous One
reveals the emptiness
of the five skandas.
O Bhagavati*,
Words fail.
Your Love alone lights the moon!

*Bhagavati is Bhagavati Maha Prajnaparamita, the Great Wisdom Mother, Mother of all Buddhas. The five skandas are Buddha's ways of categorizing what makes up the mind.

Bound

Bound
seeking three
seeking two
seeking one
Alas!
Found none!
Ahhhhh . . .
The bliss of freedom
blossoms
out of nothing!

Seer

Be the Seer
Watch . . .
The need to be seen
Vanishes

Lured

Lured by the throb of your Name
I followed you into the great beyond . . .
Namer and named
Caller and called
Merge in mystery.

Desire

The yogi
seeing all desires
arising from the One
desiring to know
Itself
drops every
thing.
Seeking only
the One
reunites with
Itself.

O Mata Kali Kundalini

O Mata Kali,
beyond speech, beyond thought,
without your grace
we're forever lost.
Out of pure Love
You planted the seed
of true knowing,
within every being!

O Mother of All,
You are Shakti Kundalini
dancing as every being,
every cell,
every atom of existence!

Awakening from potentiality to Reality
Uncoiling from your Lord
You leap to Unity Consciousness
Drawing our awareness back
into the ineffable Divine Embrace!
At last, we come to know
what can't be said,
beyond mind,
your luminous Grace.

He came down from the mountain

He came down from the mountain
conveying to his people
as best he could
the flaming Presence
I AM
but only that which
fit in words
was received by most,
except one dear soul,
awash in Love
enflamed by Adoration
she knew what was required.
The glow from the mountaintop
beckoned her in the predawn hours.

Much later the people discovered
she was nowhere to be found.
Looking to the mountain
they saw a tiny patch of red,
her scarf
nearing the shrouded summit
the faint glow of the One
barely visible.
Rushing to the base of the mountain
they were stunned by Magnificence!
Infinite Effulgence
Pure Presence,
all became still
no sound

no movement
even time ceased.

A flash of Light
a cry of ecstasy
she was gone
in an instant of Glory!

The River Flows

The river flows to the ocean
on a bed that supports its very existence.
We look at the flowing waters
oblivious to the essential underlying
foundation of its existence.
The river of thoughts and feelings
we take ourselves to be—
upon what bedrock of existence
do they flow to the sea?
The relentless stream of "I"
becoming this and that
moment by fleeting moment,
rests on the eternal awareness
the ocean of pure Being
AHAM—I AM

Practices

Practices are for the mind
this mind
in service
of all minds
Practice arises
out of no practice
root of all practice
Practice and practitioner
dissolve

The well-baked pot
no longer needs
the kiln
emptiness within
emptiness without
Abiding in
Loving-Knowing-Wisdom Awareness
No other exists.

Projections

The you at which your lover
throws their daggers
is no more you
than s/he is
the cause of your misery.

You are a fiction,
a contrivance of convention,
as is any other,
yet you will repair
this illusion day and night
defending this ghost
against non-existence.

Of all the dances
you two could choose,
like puppets
in your trances,
you let anger and fear
trample all
that is most dear.

In becoming
you've become
suffering.
In suffering
you inflict suffering.

My dear,
cease becoming
cease suffering
cease inflicting suffering.
Simply Be
Silent
Still
Free
Emaho!

Living in the mind

Living in the mind
is living in a continuous
compare and contrast tension.
Now vs past
Now vs future
Now vs ideal
Now vs I want
What is vs what should be.
This is the nature of the
constantly craving mind
born of lack, want, need and greed.
Give up your apartment
in this city of delusion!
Enter the palace of Divine Presence
Your home!
Your birthright!

Infinite Radiance

I awoke at 3am full of energy and found myself in an infinite cloud of pure Light, rays emanating in all directions, everywhere I looked. The Light was all Self, all-inclusive, illuminating the entire physical world and all transcendent domains with Self-aware, pure luminosity. This body and mind are a ray of it, as is everything. It was overwhelmingly, unspeakably beautiful. This mind wondered about whether it should go back to sleep, it didn't matter, Consciousness was beyond waking and dreaming, ecstatically radiant, illuminating all, leaving the mind literally awestruck. Eventually this body needed to get up to go to the bathroom. Eyes open, lamp turned on, putting feet on the floor, the Infinite Radiance illuminated the ordinary world in the same way. It didn't matter that a little "I" got up and relieved itself, came back to bed, and remained in the infinite expanse of Light/ Love/Consciousness. Eventually the experiencer merged with the experience and no more can be spoken of it.

Awareness shifted, back in the ordinary world I got up to go to my temple room to chant and meditate as I do each morning. I was overwhelmed with love, tears streamed down my face while doing puja to Lord Shiva and Mahadevi. I chanted for a half hour and slid back into the profound stillness and silence of the Divine embrace.

After a while, I could see the radiant expanse above and exquisite butterflies of pure light, trailing light would descend from the Infinite field of Light into the night sky. They were pure thoughts reflecting pure knowing, pure wisdom, pure Oneness. Overwhelmed by the beauty, I dissolved in tears seeing and feeling their glorious presence. After a while I became aware of a dense darker field below with heavy strands emerging and falling back into the dark field. This appeared to symbolize the mind and the dense thoughts that simply cannot rise to the level of the Radiant One or the pure wisdom thoughts created by the One to connect the lower realm to Itself and lift the poor mind from its quagmire. The butterflies of light gently swooped down and helped uplift and clarify the dense strands. Such an exquisite play of light and shadow we live in! All equally Divine!

Other

O mind,
you see yourself as other
projecting otherness everywhere.
You are a product of the veil of otherness.
It is all you perceive
until Grace
lifts Her veil
dissolving your separateness
in the sweet union
of the Divine Embrace!
Ahhhh . . .
the rapturous ecstasy
of resting in the fullness
of infinite Being
embracing all as Divine Self,
home at last
the mind/other ceases,
unshakeable peace remains.

Silence deepening

Silence deepening
Squeezing
Releasing all energy
Out of sound

Listen
Listen deeply
More deeply

Beyond speech
Beyond sound
Beyond silence

Listen
Silence
Revealing
Sound
Emerging from Light

Infinite Light
Radiance beyond imagining
Throbbing brilliance
Pulsing all-embracing Light
All-embracing Love
Divine Presence
Self-revealing
Self-knowing

Silent Seer
Never seen
Known only by those
Who disappear.

Scavenging

Mata Kundalini,
You want only to
Reveal our unbreakable
Unity with all—
All creatures
All creation
And the One beyond
All thought.

While mind and body
Scavenge for fallen fruit,
The only kind
Within their reach,
You dissolve the bonds
Of misidentification
Constraining consciousness
To states of
Waking, dream and deep sleep.

Your sword of discrimination
Clears all that obscures
Our Oneness
Our boundless Being
Our boundless Consciousness
Our boundless Rapture
Our boundless Love.

Knowing this to be
Our true nature
By your Grace,
All cravings cease
All anger evaporates
The sun of Loving Compassion
Illumines all as our Self.

either/or

O mind
You live in a tiny world
of either/or.
God's world is
all this and more!
all this and more!

Fractured

Spiritual practices
heal and unite
fractured parts

When a thorn pierces
your finger
it bleeds.
Your wholeness isn't broken
you don't neglect
to care for your finger.
Parts of you,
cells of skin and blood
are dying
but not your sense
of wholeness,
which embraces
the wounded part,
cleans the wound,
protects it
safeguarding its healing.

Your Divine wholeness
offers its grace through practices,
wisdom and Love,
bandaging your wounds,
healing your splintered self,
and reacquainting you
with your Divine wholeness
your eternal Self.

O novelty seeking mind

O novelty seeking mind
you are a magpie
chasing shiny objects
seeking your fantasies
of the Infinite One,
in your imaginings
of what the One is,
in your imaginings
of what meditation is.

Just as you don't notice
the space that holds all
from threads of energy
to all the galaxies in the universe
you don't see the One
fully present here and now,
always here and now!
Look around!
Your foot touching the ground,
your face in the mirror,
the traffic outside,
the breath coming in and going out,
emotions rising and subsiding,
the news of fools barking mad for power,
the compassion of a chef feeding millions,
ALL SHIVA!
Nashivam vidyate qua chit!
THERE IS NOTHING THAT IS NOT SHIVA!

When living for Love

When living for Love
is more important than
living for profits,
when living in Love
is more important
than living in power,
when living in communion with all
is more important than
living to exploit all,
when living in Love every moment
dissolves the delusion of separation,
then living joyously
in Love with all
becomes all
liberating all.
Emaho!

Only One

O my Beloved,
when will humanity
be free of suffering?

My dear One,
When individuals see
as I see
Oneness, no other
Only One
Only One
they know the rapture
    of true freedom
    indivisible union.
When all humanity evolves
    to see Oneness
    to see all creation as their Self
    knowing that to harm another
    is to harm yourself,
Then suffering will cease.

Many of my emissaries throughout time
have proclaimed this truth,
this golden rule, in words so simple all can understand:
    Confucius—"do not do to others what you wouldn't
want done to yourself."
    Christ—"do unto others as you would have them
do unto you."
The truth is THERE ARE NO OTHERS!
AHAM encompasses all!

My dearest Beloved

My dearest Beloved,
entering the deepest recesses
of the cave of our heart,
the heart of creation,
we leave the waking world
each night to enter
true wakefulness,
silently swirling, merging,
Light entwined with Light,
not even the playful illusion
of two remains!

A new dawn!
Dharma calls!
What miracles of Light-born forms
will you parade before me today,
my dearest Beloved!
Light becoming light!
Light becoming sound!
Light becoming mind!
Light becoming body!
Luminous Love becoming all!
Light giving forms to adore!
Light, my dearest Beloved,
Your Light
even becoming me!
Rapturous play!
Ecstatic dance!
'til we retreat once again
to the cave of our heart,

Light embracing Light
merging beyond Light,
Love
Love birthing Light
Light merging in Love
Love dissolving all.

The Truth Is One

The Truth is one
the beginning is silent
the end is silent
the revelation—beyond words . . .
My Beloved,
why so many practices, teachings, religions, paths?

My dear One,
The novelty seeking,
entertainment craving,
reactive mind,
keeps looking everywhere
for what already lies within!
I must plant hints and signs
all over my creation
to get its attention!
Turn within, turn within!
All is revealed
in not seeking,
not doing,
not thinking,
simply BEING,
silent and free
the union of
you and ME!

I am the One

I am the One
    appearing as many
I am the Boundless
    ocean of Compassion
I am the Unfathomable
    sea of Love
I am the Unshakeable
    mountain of Peace
I am all that is
    and all that isn't
None can say what I AM
    nor what I am not
I AM
AHAM
I AM
AHAM
I AM
AHAM

You opened my eyes!

O my Beloved,
You opened my eyes!
Seeing you everywhere
rejoicing in You
becoming anything and everything
to lure us back to
Your sublime embrace!
Mantras and yantras,
prayers and practices,
beauty and awe,
even mind-stopping terror,
corralling the mind,
calling out to Your rays of Light—
Remember your Source
Remember you are One
Remember you are LOVE
Remember!
Now!

Radiant Kali

The blinding blackness
of your mysterious radiance,
my Beloved,
vanquishes all who are blessed
by Your summons,
as grace leads them
to You for final release.
From your infinite ocean of ecstasy
waves of rapture lap at the shores of the mind
carrying it away babbling
about unspeakable union.
You drench the body
with your juicy Love nectar
as it trembles and screams
O Kali! Kali! Kali!
in your passionate embrace!
Now,
all has returned to Source
leaving not a trace.

Open Heart

Our Beloved asked
What can hold me?
Not the earth!
Not the stars!
Not boundless space itself!
Ahhhh, but a pure
Open heart
Holds all the Love
I am.

Rise

The new-day sun
 rises over the ocean,
Luminous mist
 drifts ashore
enveloping me
 in a cloud of light.

Walking into the radiant mist,
 becoming the mist
I rise
into the sun-drenched sky.

Becoming sky
filled with light
I rise
into space,
 becoming space
 infinite, all-embracing

I rise
into Consciousness,
 becoming pure Consciousness
 everything and nothing all at once

I hold all
All is born
Within me.

O my beloved Shiva

O my beloved Shiva,
my radiant Self,
caressing my entire body
all of creation
I play at your feet.
Our ecstatic dance
of silence and stillness
appears to be ceaselessly
flowing, erupting, subsiding, birthing . . .
infinite universes come and go
never exhausting our creativity
our ecstasy!

Our beloved creatures know
but a tiny fleeting speck
of our Being, Consciousness and Bliss.
Most live fully enthralled by the dance,
not seeking more.
Our beloved humans
we've endowed with the longing to know
driving them onward through countless
lives before they finally discover
what they truly need, what they truly long for,
what the knowing of which
delivers them from suffering,
opening the door to radical freedom
reuniting with me, Mother of All!
Incomparably blissful reunion!

The release of eons of longing,
eons of suffering, erased in an instant
of rapturous Love!

In the brief time they've walked the earth
humans have repeatedly gotten lost
following their delusions about what
will satisfy the longing I gave them
as a homing beacon!
I gave them a bit of my creativity
and they keep using it to wander off
leaving more suffering in their wake!

I keep sending emissaries,
spirit animals, sages, Confucius,
Lao Tzu, Buddhas, Christs,
saints, poets, artists, composers
yantras, mantras, tantras!
Every sense is a portal to rapture!
I even divinized sex!
Yet, they still get lost!
So driven they are by fear and attraction,
ephemeral irrelevancies,
power, domination and exploitation . . .
they don't hold onto eternal truths.
It's easier to get the wind to cease
than it is to get them to still their minds!

They need more of you, my beloved Shiva!
They need your detachment
your unshakeable equanimity
your all-embracing Consciousness
Witnessing without becoming

Seer who is never seen!
The One who sees only His Beloved!
Yet, when I give you a form
for them to adore and delight in,
they turn it into a religion
creating more differences and strife!

What's a mother to do?

Listening

Entering silence
we become more
and more transparent
Silence dissolving thoughts
Silence dissolving mind
Silence dissolving filters
that distort and block
the ineffable.
Listen
feel ever deeper into
the mystery of silence
stillness
Listen
free from commentary
free from interpretation
free from self
listener dissolving
into listening
Listen
beyond hearing
Listen
transparent to mystery
Listen
naked presence
unknowing, unsought
Listen

Tell me

Tell me
how do you relate
to a diamond's brilliance?
How do you relate
to the exquisite all-pervasive Light?
Like a flower, perhaps,
offering every tender petal?

O the yearning!
O the burning!
Naked
Exposed
Offering all darkness,
every hidden recess,
begging to be entered,
penetrated by Love,
caressed by Love,
bathed in Love,
made wholly transparent
by this Light of Love!
Love alone
Love alone
Love alone
IS!

Buddhas and bodhisattvas everywhere

Buddhas and bodhisattvas everywhere
Yet suffering remains.
The blind craving mind
Alone is to blame.
Spinning on its pedestal of ignorance,
Forever bound by the same,
If what you truly seek
Is freedom for all
This deluded mind
You must tame!

You are a hammer

O mind,
as tools go
you are a hammer
shattering the One
magnificent diamond
of Divine creation
to bits,
while complaining
that the broken shards
amount to nothing.

Mind Maze

You are hopelessly lost
in a mirrored mind maze
Subsisting on
mirage water
as you chase about,
unconscious of seeing
only reflections
of your own
deluded self.
There are no others.
Even I am your projection.
What am I as you
or you as I
trying to communicate
to no other?

Know the inexhaustible fullness

Know the inexhaustible fullness
of simply Being.
Bring that to your relationships.
Fullness of Being is boundless Love.
Don't expect relationships
to give you fullness of Being.
It lies within.

Know the inexhaustible fullness
of simply Being.
Fullness of Being is boundlessly creative.
Bring that to your life and work
and these will be
expressions of your fullness
not an antidote to your emptiness.

Know the inexhaustible fullness
of simply Being
every moment of every day
the flow of time
the river of grace
ever revealing
new facets of
our Beloved's face!

AHAM

AHAM
I AM
This is the root
and the flower
of all practices.
This is the truth
of who you are.
Pure Awareness
of Infinite BEING
Suffused with boundless
Love, Compassion, Wisdom and Rapture!
Never forget the Rapture, my dear!
AHAM

My beloved Shakti

My beloved Shakti,
you delight equally
in becoming and dissolving,
concealing and revealing!
You dance as mind,
atomizer of the One,
cloaking boundless Unity
you play as infinite forms.
Mind is your instrument
Mind is your music
Mind is your paint brush
Mind is your paint
Mind is your clay
Mind is your kiln
All galaxies, stars and planets
Emerge from your fire!
All creatures, beings and thoughts
Coalesce from your cloud of Light Energy—
You my beloved Shakti!
Dancing as all that is!
You are Consciousness
embracing and birthing all
within your Self!
Mysteries beyond mysteries
this humbled mind
takes refuge
in silence
at your feet.

My Lord

My Lord,
I longed to see
Your unadorned face,
You beckoned me into
the cloud of unknowing,
silently you drew me
past all that is suffering
all that is bound
all that is glorious
all that is numinous
into Your infinite heart
where I and Thou
ceased to exist,
the unspeakable
alone
is

Your Ferocious Grace

O my beloved Kali,
Your radiant blackness
illumines this dark age,
Your ferocious grace
is the medicine
that cures the disease
of the deluded mind
ravaging the world
and all beings!

Your ferocious grace
drowns suffering
in your roiling ocean of
self-annihilating Love!

Your ferocious grace,
burning with the light
of a thousand suns,
destroys the darkness of ignorance,
only the numinous state
of unity beyond words remains!

Dear friend,
take refuge in Ma Kali!
Om Kali Ma!
Om Kali Ma!
Om Kali Ma!
She will purge the
inner and outer worlds
of all pain and suffering

'til only Love,
Only Love,
eternal, boundless Love
embracing all
is known
by all!

Jai Maa!

Tea

My dear friend,
You may enjoy
many flavors of tea,
however, you can live
without the tea,
but not without the water.

You may enjoy
many flavors of the Divine's wisdom
steeped in one religion
or another,
but have you drunk
the pure nectar,
the Divine essence
that gives birth to all religions
before it has been colored
and flavored
by the limited minds
and words of others—
priests, rabbis, swamis,
monks, teachers, masters
or even your own mind?

The wellspring of Infinite Wisdom,
Love, Compassion, Rapture and Creativity,
what some call God,
or Goddess
or Buddha
or Tara . . .
forever flows within you

as you
as your life
as all beings
as all creation!

Leave behind all minds!
All religions!
Silently enter
the holiest temple of all,
the heart
your heart,
know the pristine
pure Presence
of the eternal One
forever residing within you.

Giving Thanks

Grateful hearts rejoice!
Celebrating abundance
Give all to all, now!

Holiday Blessing

May you revel in the luminous gifts of grace
This holiday season!

May you know the Love of the One
That dissolves all differences.

May you know the Love of the One
That embraces all with compassion.

May you know the Love of the One
That infuses you with steady Wisdom.

May you know the Love of the One
That bestows unshakeable Peace.

May you know the Love of the One
Taking birth now in your heart.

New Year Blessing

As the old year comes to a close
May you deeply inhale all
The gifts and blessings it brought
And exhale fully all
The pain and suffering you endured.
Let the knowledge and strength you developed
Moving through the past
be fully present as you
Greet the New Year!

May you know the living presence of the Divine
That warms and comforts your soul
Like the gentle rays of the sun
Caressing your face on a winter day.

May you feel the living presence of the Divine
In the tides of your breath, the drum beat of your heart,
The light in a loved one's eyes and the warmth of their touch.

May your presence in the world
Be a quiet reminder for others
Of God's gracious and generous presence,
For you carry the One in your heart
Wherever you go, whether you know it or not.

May you tread your path through time
Leaving footprints of love, compassion, and wisdom.

May you greet the New Year
With wonder and delight
And the courage born of knowing
The Divine's embrace
At all times,
In every place.

Blessed Mother

O Beloved Mary,
Give us the joyful
loving surrender
with which you
carried the Divine
into this world.

Who but you,
Holy Mother,
Great Goddess,
Spouse of the
Nameless One,
could bear the
the excruciating pain
and never cease
embracing all
in Love?

Who but you
can birth the
Light of the Divine
into forms we
can approach?

You've watched
Your creation,
born of pure Love,
destroyed by those
proudly proclaiming
their deluded fantasies,

reeking of ignorance,
fear, anger, and greed.

How, my beloved Mother,
do you continue
to hold your loving arms
open to these
murderous villains
ravaging your exquisite
earthly body,
destroying entire species,
habitats and cultures,
as these greedy black holes
devour all they encounter?

O my Beloved,
the power of your
Loving presence
alone
can fill the emptiest soul,
healing the excruciating pain
those who haven't known
Your love endure.

Ever present,
Ever giving,
Known by countless names
You pour yourself,
Your Loving presence
into any who turn
to You!

What can we do
to serve, my Beloved?
Remind people to
take refuge in You,
abide in You,
trust You are
already holding
them in Your
Loving embrace.

O sweet soul,
you're safe now,
inhale Her Love,
let go into Her,
rest in your Beloved,
let Her graceful loving presence
dissolve all your burdens,
all your dis-ease,
empowering you to
live Love
into your world.

Only The One

The blessings of the Infinite
flowing through countless
Goddesses and Gods
buddhas and bodhisattvas
sages and saints
poured over this encrusted mind
for lifetimes beyond imagining
clearing my vision
'til I could see at last
the world is a mirror
reflecting only the One!

My dear friend

My dear friend,
If someone locked you in a museum,
no matter how fascinating the displays may be,
you would still be imprisoned.

Don't lock yourself in a religious system,
a museum of past revelations.
The Infinite One is revealing Herself
right here, right now!
Always here and now!

Many have dissolved into Her loving embrace
never having heard of the Divine Mother.

Many have dissolved in the pristine emptiness
radiant with boundless compassion, wisdom, joy, and peace,
never having heard of Buddha.

Many have come face to face with God the Father
never having known of Jesus.

Many have drowned in the ocean of surrender,
love and mercy
never having known of Mohammed.

Many have known the self-erasing sea of Love,
felt the truth of "ein od milvado"*,
never having studied Torah.

The Divine is Infinite!
Infinite in Her generosity!
Infinite in giving countless ways of knowing
your Divine Source,
here and now,
Always here and now!

There—in the sky—see!
There—in the stream—see!
There—in that person—see!
There—in that wonder—see!
There—in that joy—see!
There—in that pain—see!
There—in your heart—see!
See!
See!
See!
Her ever-active power of revelation
illumines the true Reality
every moment!
See!
Rejoice!

*Ancient Jewish mantra: "there is nothing that is not God!"

Om Kali Ma

Serving Kali
Kalidas disappeared
Only Ma
remains.

Reality

Finite
Infinite
Figure
Ground
Both
Neither
Awareness all-encompassing
Awareness unbound!

You love loving God

You love loving God,
You delight in praising God,
You find peace in worshipping God,
You thoroughly enjoy serving God.
Grace has descended upon you
and made this possible.

Grace now calls you to go beyond,
beyond loving God,
beyond praising God,
beyond worshipping God,
beyond the joy of serving God.
God's grace has descended upon you,
calling you to merge in God,
lover and Beloved
united as One.
See
truly see
God loving God!
God praising God!
God worshipping God!
God serving God!

The Way Beyond The Way

Follow the way beyond the way.
Practice with love and enthusiasm.
Practice with discipline and perseverance.
Follow the path to the end of the path.
Follow the sound to the end of sound.
Follow the light to the end of light.
Follow time to the end of time.
Om Kali Ma
Portal beyond all . . .
Enter where there's no entry.
Go 'til there's no more going.
Nothing—everything—gone.
Annihilated by the terrible truth
There is no path, no truth,
Nothing
No one traversing a path
Nothing
Gaté gaté paragaté parasamgaté bodhi swaha!

'til then
Follow the way beyond the way.
Practice with love and enthusiasm.
Practice with discipline and perseverance.
Follow the path to the end of the path.

You utterly consumed me

You utterly consumed me,
You, known by Dante,
You, the Love that moves
the sun and stars,
You, the One who is All,
You, AHAM.

This one is no poet

This one is no poet,
barely a mirage of a portal
is all that remains!
What radiates through
this liminal apparition,
words and mantras,
thangkas and yantras,
emanations of the Self of all,
your Self,
embraces all
in the Light of Loving Wisdom.
All there is,
is You, my dear,
All Love.

That which never was

That which never was
continues,
Illuminated by
that which alone
eternally
is.

Video Links

Deep Longing: The Mystics' Way
https://youtu.be/c9HAW8wcxv0

Lovely little snowflake
https://youtu.be/jYARdNOsF28

Who Can Say What I'm Not—chant
https://youtu.be/H_4EQztqmV4

About The Author

Lawrence Edwards grew up in the suburbs of New York City. His mystical experiences that first began as a young child led him to the formal study of meditation and psychology in undergraduate and graduate school. He graduated magna cum laude in 1974 from the University of Connecticut. During this time, he practiced meditation and hatha yoga and began studying Tibetan Buddhism with Chogyam Trungpa Rinpoche. He continued practicing and studying in Buddhist and yogic traditions, which culminated in his training as to be a monk under the direct guidance of his Kundalini meditation master in India. He went on to earn a PhD from Temple University in 1986. His doctoral research was on delineating the types of psychological change and spiritual growth experienced through the long-term practice of a Kundalini-based yoga. Kundalini Shakti is the ancient yogic term for the innate universal power of Consciousness, transformation and revelation, which is the root of all forms of yoga. Later he received teachings and empowerments from H.H. the Dalai Lama, H.E. Tsewong Sitar Rinpoche, and Gelek Rinpoche.

In addition to practicing and teaching meditation for more than fifty years, Dr. Edwards is trained in Jungian depth psychology, biofeedback and neurofeedback, and was board certified in neuro-biofeedback (BCIA senior fellow). He has served on the board of directors and as president of the Northeast Regional Biofeedback Society. As a New York state licensed psychotherapist (LMHC), Dr. Edwards was in private practice offering transpersonal psychotherapy for more than thirty years, and served on the faculty of New York Medical College for twenty-four years.

Dr. Edwards is the founder and director of Anam Cara Meditation, an educational organization that he started right after the 9/11 terrorist attacks, which had such a devastating impact on his suburban New York community and beyond. With the mission of Anam Cara (ancient Gaelic for "friend of the soul") to make the powerful transformative practices of meditation freely available to all, Dr. Edwards has offered free bi-weekly meditation programs, and online resources, in addition to retreats and courses, for more than two decades. He continues to work with individuals and groups interested in deepening their meditation practices and spiritual development.

For more information, please visit:
www.anamcarameditation.org and www.thesoulsjourney.com

Other critically acclaimed writings by Lawrence Edwards include:
The Soul's Journey: Guidance From The Divine Within (2000)
Awakening Kundalini: The Path To Radical Freedom (2013)
Kali's Bazaar Penned by Kalidas (2012)
O My Beloved: Whisperings From The Divine Heard By Kalidas (2022)

www.ingramcontent.com/pod-product-compliance
Lightning Source LLC
Chambersburg PA
CBHW030249130626
46549CB00002B/451